Myths of
West
AFRICA

Bridget Giles

RAINTREE
STECK-VAUGHN
PUBLISHERS

A Harcourt Company

Austin   New York

Steck-Vaughn Company
First published 2002 by Raintree Steck-Vaughn Publishers, an imprint of Steck-Vaughn Company.

© 2002 Brown Partworks Limited

Library of Congress Cataloging-in-Publication Data

Giles, Bridget.
    Myths of west Africa / Bridget Giles.
        p. cm. -- (Mythic world)
    Includes bibliographical references and index.
    ISBN 0-7398-4976-X

Printed and bound in the United States
1 2 3 4 5 6 7 8 9 0 IP 05 04 03 02 01

Series Consultant: C. Scott Littleton, Professor of Anthropology,
Occidental College, Los Angeles
Volume Author: Bridget Giles

for Brown Partworks Limited
Project Editor: Lee Stacy
Designer: Sarah Williams
Picture Researcher: Helen Simm
Cartographer: Mark Walker
Indexer: Kay Ollerenshaw
Managing Editor: Tim Cooke
Design Manager: Lynne Ross
Production Manager: Matt Weyland

for Raintree Steck-Vaughn
Project Editor: Sean Dolan
Production Manager: Richard Johnson

Contents

General Introduction

MYTHS ARE THE MIRRORS of humanity. They reflect the inner soul of a culture and try to give profound answers in a seemingly mysterious world. In other words, myths give the relevant culture an understanding of its place in the world and the universe in general. Found in all civilizations, myths sometimes combine fact and fiction and other times are complete fantasy. Regardless of their creative origin, myths are always dramatic.

Every culture has its own myths, yet globally there are common themes and symbols, even across civilizations that had no contact with or awareness of each other. Some of the most common types include those that deal with the creation of the world, the cosmos, or a particular site, like a large mountain or lake. Other myths deal with the origin of humans, or a specific people or civilization, or the heroes or gods who either made the world inhabitable or gave humans something essential, such as the ancient Greek Titan Prometheus, who gave fire, or the Ojibwa hero Wunzh, who was given divine instructions on cultivating corn. There are also myths about the end of the world, death and the afterlife, and the renewal or change of seasons.

The origin of evil and death are also common themes. Examples of such myths are the Biblical Eve eating the forbidden fruit or the ancient Greek story of Pandora opening the sealed box.

Additionally there are flood myths, myths about the sun and the moon, and myths of a peaceful, beautiful place of reward, such as heaven or Elysium, or of punishment, such as hell or Tartarus. Myths also teach important human values, such as courage. In all cases, myths show that the gods and their deeds are outside of ordinary human life and yet essential to it.

In this volume some of the best known West African myths are presented, as well as a few that are not so well known. Following each myth is an explanation of how the myth was either reflected in or linked to the real life of West Africans. There is also a glossary at the end of the volume to help identify the major mythological and historical characters as well as explain many cultural terms.

MYTHOLOGY OF WEST AFRICA

The myths of West Africa are as diverse and varied as its people. Thousands of languages are spoken in the region, and many different religions are followed. Each group of people has their own sets of myths, and the details of the stories can vary within groups depending who is retelling them. Myths also change over the centuries as the culture that created them evolves. Some stories spread to other regions and are adopted by different ethnic groups, each of whom adapts them for their own purposes. All these factors have created a large and diverse body of mythology.

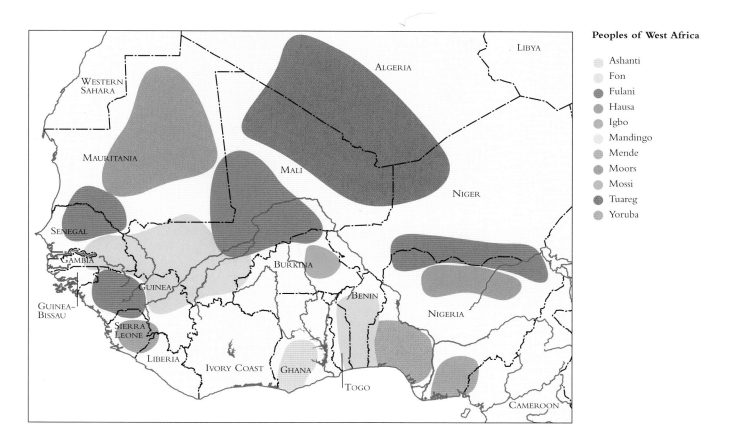

Peoples of West Africa

- Ashanti
- Fon
- Fulani
- Hausa
- Igbo
- Mandingo
- Mende
- Moors
- Mossi
- Tuareg
- Yoruba

Studying the myths of West Africa can reveal some surprises. To many people, myths are typically the stories of religions whose followers, such as the ancient Greeks or Romans, are long since dead. Yet many West African myths are integral parts of modern-day faiths, such as the Yoruba and Igbo religions, whose followers are still thriving and number in the many thousands. In such cases the boundaries between myth and religion are blurred and frequently change. Like religion, mythology need not be static and unchanging, and African myths reflect this.

Over 1,000 years ago many West Africans began adopting religions such as Islam and Christianity. Traditional African religions are still widely followed, however, often as well as the world faiths. African myths reflect this diversity, with elements of Christianity and Islam interwoven with African religions. Some myths, such as that on pages 18–19 about Seku Ahmadu

Above: *Highlighted in this color-coded map are the locations of the major cultures in West Africa. The area covers nearly 2.4 million sq. miles (6 million sq. km).*

and Waada Samba, may try to resolve the contradictions between seemingly opposing sets of beliefs. In turn, African myths have spread around the globe, traveling as far afield as the Americas, where they have spawned their own traditions, which are uniquely American but retain an African sentiment.

Myths are not just about religion and spiritual beliefs. They are also told to entertain and to educate, and this is especially true of West Africa. Young children are taught what is acceptable behavior as they listen to the mishaps and adventures of mythical characters, and historic events and figures are remembered and preserved in their myths, which are retold at special occasions and other events, serving as unique history lessons.

Iyadola's Babies

People's myths explain the world around them. West Africa is a region of diverse peoples, cultures, languages, and religions. This Igbo myth relates how all people were created by Iyadola, the Earth Mother.

IN THE BEGINNING, there was only sky and barren earth. Nyame, who is also called the Sky God, was lonely in the clouds. One day, he filled a calabash (a container made from a gourd) with plants and animals, then ripped a huge hole in the sky. Nyame lowered the calabash containing his creations to the earth, where they flourished and multiplied. From then on the Sky God no longer felt lonely, with lions, elephants, monkeys, birds, and other animals to watch for him on earth.

Inside Nyame lived two spirit people, a man and a woman. They, too, liked to watch events unfold beneath them and would creep to Nyame's lip to peer out of his mouth. One day Nyame gave a terrific sneeze and the pair flew out of his mouth, landing on the ground far below. Unable to return to the sky, they made themselves at home. The man learned how to kill animals with sharpened sticks, and he often left the woman, Iyadola, alone at home while he went hunting.

Iyadola grew more and more lonely. One day, she had an idea. "If I find clay and make some little people and bake them in the fire, they could be our children," Iyadola mused. "Then I would not be lonely anymore." Later, she convinced her husband that they should try to put her idea into practice. The next day, he helped her make a whole batch of little clay children. They carefully placed their creations in the warm embers of a fire. Suddenly, they heard the Sky God crashing through the forest and shouting their names. Terrified that their creations would anger him, Iyadola and her husband plucked them from the fire and hid them. When Nyame reached their clearing, he asked what the fire was for. "To keep us warm," they replied.

The Sky God was suspicious, but he left them alone for the time being. Iyadola and her husband made several batches of clay children that day, but Nyame kept returning without warning when they tried to bake them. Some batches had to be taken out of the fire before they were ready, and others were overcooked. Finally, night came and Nyame returned to the sky. Iyadola laid her creations out on the forest floor. Some of the children were almost white because they were not cooked properly. Others had been burned black. Some were yellow, brownish red, or pink. Pleased with the results, Iyadola breathed life into her children. They opened their eyes, wriggled their feet, and were soon playing in the forest. Iyadola, who is also known as the Earth Mother, was never lonely again.

Above: *Iyadola, the first woman, molded clay figures then baked them in a fire. The longer the figures were cooked the darker they became. For the believers in the myth, this crowded marketplace in Timbuktu, Mali, shows the descendants of some of Iyadola's dark clay figures.*

Languages and People of West Africa

West Africa is a region of great diversity, both culturally and linguistically. Around 700 different languages are spoken in West Africa, more than nearly any other region in the world.

West Africa, where the Igbo myth of Iyadola and her clay children originates, takes up a vast chunk of the world's second-largest continent. There is no one correct way to define West Africa (see map on page 5), but it generally includes all the countries enclosed by Mauritania, Mali, Niger, and Cameroon, including those countries themselves. From north to south, West Africa can be divided into very rough geographic zones: the southwestern parts of the Sahara Desert and the semidesert Sahel, which fringes the desert's south; grasslands; highlands; forests; and, on the coast, long sandy beaches and mangrove swamps.

The people of West Africa, like Iyadola's clay children, are even more diverse than the landscape. It is common to divide African peoples into "tribes," but this term is misleading. It is not really appropriate for groups of people that number in the millions and have histories

Left: *A Ghanaian chief at an annual festival in Ghana. The modern state of Ghana is located on the southern coast of West Africa. The ancient West African empire was sited farther north.*

stretching back thousands of years. People are divided into these so-called tribes, or ethnic groups, according to the language they speak, the history they share, and often also the religion they practice. Since all these features change over the centuries, as people adapt and borrow elements from each other's culture, ethnic groups are flexible concepts that are often more recent than people realize.

The vast majority of West Africans are black Africans but an important minority are not; they include Arabs from North Africa and farther afield, as well as Europeans and Asians. Many black Africans, such as the Fang of Gabon, speak languages that belong to the huge Bantu group of languages.

Bantu-speakers were the first iron workers in Africa, and they probably originated from somewhere in the great forests between the Niger and Congo rivers in western Africa. Over thousands of years, family groups gradually migrated out from the heartland, perhaps moving only a few miles a generation.

Many other West Africans speak languages described as semi-Bantu, including the Yoruba, Ashanti, and the Mande-speaking people. The Bambara, Malinke, Mandingo, and Mende people all speak Mande languages. Others, such as the Hausa of northern Nigeria, speak languages that are more closely related to East African and Middle Eastern languages. People such as the Fulani, the Moors of Mauritania, and the Tuareg who, respectively, have African, Arabic, and Berber ancestors, speak languages that reflect their history.

WEST AFRICAN LIFESTYLES

Most West Africans make their living by farming or raising animals, but many West Africans live and work in towns and cities, in offices or shops, and in modern industries. Historically,

and to a lesser extent today, West Africans of certain ethnic groups have been associated with particular occupations. The Yoruba, Igbo, and many Mande peoples, for example, are still generally farmers. In the past, the majority of the Tuareg, Fulani, and Moors were nomads who lived in the desert, herding animals and trading goods with settled neighbors. Today, farmers and nomads trade goods, and it is often women who dominate the markets in West Africa.

Above: *A desert-dwelling Tuareg family dismantle their domed cloth-covered house in preparation for moving to another oasis.*

Left: *A Nigerian farmer, wearing a large straw hat for protection against the midday sun, tends a palm oil field. Palm oil is one of the region's most important crops.*

Lost and Found

The Dausi *epic poems are sung and narrated by griots (storytellers) of the Soninke people. They tell the part-mythical, part-factual history of the city of Wagadu.*

LIKE ALL EPIC POEMS, *The Dausi* are full of stories on a grand scale: heroes and heroines, great battles, and heroic deeds; the tales here are only fragments. *The Dausi*, which were first sung to a prince by a bird, reveal how Wagadu was lost to humanity four times. The first time, the city disappeared to punish the vanity of the king and his oldest son. Wagadu later reappeared but was lost again through falsehood, then greed, and finally dissension.

Wagadu's first reappearance was thanks to Lagarre, the youngest son of an old and infirm Soninke king called Mama Dinga. The king declared that if the great war drum, Tabele, were found, Wagadu would become visible again. Tabele had been stolen by jinn (or genies) and tied to the sky. Fooled into thinking that Lagarre was his eldest son, the near-blind Mama Dinga told Lagarre that if he washed in the contents of nine magical jars, he would understand the language of the jinn and all the animals.

Lagarre did as his father instructed and soon afterward a jinni appeared who told the prince to visit an ancient lizard in the forest. The lizard sent him to the jackal, who sent him to the buzzard, Kiloko. After Lagarre had fed Kiloko for 10 days, the bird was strong enough to wrench Tabele from the sky and bring it to Lagarre. When Lagarre beat the great war drum, Wagadu appeared before him.

In front of the city's gates lay a mighty snake called Bida. Kiloko had warned Lagarre that Bida would expect to be given 10 maidens every year in return for making it rain gold three times a year. Lagarre faced the coiled serpent with courage and made a new bargain with him — one maiden a year for three rainfalls of gold.

Bida agreed, and the ritual sacrifice to the serpent continued for many years until it came to be the turn of Sia Jatta Bari, the most beautiful Soninke maiden of all. Sia was in love with a nobleman called Mamadi Sefe Dekote. He swore that Wagadu would rot before he let Sia be killed by the snake Bida. On the day of the sacrifice Mamadi sharpened his sword until it could split a grain of wheat. The people of Wagadu led Sia, dressed in all her finery, to the well where Bida lived. As usual, Bida raised his head from the well three times; on the third time, Mamadi cut off the serpent's head with one stroke of his sword. As Bida's head flew through the air, these words left his mouth: "For seven years, seven months, and seven days, Wagadu will be without its golden rain." Bida's curse greatly angered the people of Wagadu, and they turned on Mamadi in rage. Mamadi swept Sia onto his horse and rode with her to safety in his mother's town. As for Bida's head, it fell far away to the south, where it became a source of much gold.

Above: *The ancient West Africans associated the wild buzzard with the mythical Kiloko, a buzzard, that was credited with retrieving Tabele, the great war drum that conjured up the city of Wagadu.*

Maintaining Oral History

Griots are more than professional storytellers: like other historians, they chronicle facts. They do so not in books but by narrating stories or performing songs, such as The Dausi, which are passed down from generation to generation.

Stories such as how Lagarre revealed Wagadu originated long before cultures began writing down stories. Such tales were and still are preserved by word of mouth, which is termed oral history. Scientific studies of ancient artifacts, languages, and documents such as traveler's accounts have proven many oral accounts to be accurate. Oral history includes praise songs, epic poems, riddles, proverbs, children's rhymes, folktales, fables, legends, and myths. Praise songs relate the exploits of local or national heroes, including politicians today. Legends and myths explain the sometimes part-factual origins of people, kings, dynasties, cities, and kingdoms.

Epic poems are long stories on a grand scale. People the world over have epic poems. The ancient Greeks had the *Iliad* and *Odyssey*, and the Anglo-Saxons, *Beowulf*. It was only recently that scholars recognized Africa had such narratives, too. More than 1,700 years ago, the Soninke people established a kingdom based around the city of Wagadu. It grew into an empire that came to be known as Ghana, which was the king's title. The history of this state is recounted in *The Dausi*. *The Dausi* are not West Africa's only epic poems. The Fulani have their own epics, called *Baudi*, which relate their history.

Left: *A modern griot entertains a crowd with ancient and modern stories. The people are gathered in a village near Accra, the capital of Ghana.*

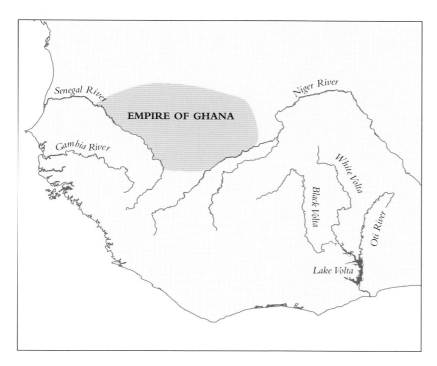

There are epic poems about many other historic West African states, including the medieval empires of Songhay and Mali. An interesting feature of African epic poems is how the wording and other details can vary at each telling, according to the imagination of the teller, while the story still follows the correct plot.

ORAL HISTORIANS

Griots are known by various different names in West Africa, depending on their mother tongue. Women and men can be griots, and all have mastered the art of public speaking or singing. They usually learn their craft from their mother or father, and many also travel to study with more experienced experts.

In West Africa griots are important storers and transmitters of oral history. They often hold positions of respect in their communities, and are invited to

Above: *The extent of the ancient empire of Ghana in A.D. 1000.*

Right: *The Guinean author Camara Laye (1928–1980) was one of the first writers from West Africa to gain an international reputation. His novels, such as* The Radiance of the King, *continue the storyteller tradition, but on the page rather than spoken.*

perform at weddings, funerals, naming ceremonies, and other celebrations. Griots reach all levels of society, and they hold recitals in family homes, market places, and royal courts.

Performing solo or accompanied by musicians and singers, a griot might tell the history of one particular family to which he or she is attached or relate a national history. A griot's performance should both educate and entertain. In such ways, the whole community learns the history of their people.

Griots often travel widely for their work, spreading recent news and current events as well as more ancient histories. During World War II (1939–1945), for example, griots brought news of successful campaigns in North Africa to West African countries south of the Sahara Desert in a matter of days.

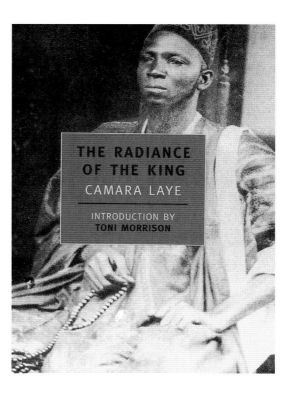

Seven Sons for Seven Virgins

Tuareg traders once dominated large parts of the Sahara Desert. They also roamed the dry grasslands of the Sahel in what are now northern Niger and Mali in West Africa and southern Algeria and Libya in North Africa.

ALTHOUGH THEY HAVE been Muslim for many centuries, the Tuareg have myths that date from before Muhammad, the founder of Islam. These ancient Tuareg myths tell of spirit founders. Thousands of years ago, a people called the Gaawo lived in a vast desert country. One year, the Gaawo were attacked and defeated by a tribe made up of a strange race of people. Every year following their defeat, the Gaawo people had to pay tribute to their conquerors by sending them seven virgins who would become brides for the young men of the ruling tribe.

Usually, the seven Gaawo virgins were sent on their long journey across the desert alone, but one year the elders decided that a wise man should accompany the young women. Spirits called jinn (or genies) lived in the desert, and they might harm the virgins before they completed their journey. The Gaawo feared that if the virgins did not reach their destination safely then there might be harsh reprisals from their rulers. The man the elders chose to travel with the women was an old marabout, a Muslim holy man of great wisdom and learning.

Riding on camels, the group of travelers set out early one morning — it was far too hot in the desert to travel in the middle of the day. After a long day's journey, they reached a valley. On the valley floor, they could see a patch of green interrupting the sand dunes and dry plains. Palm trees and figs grew in the lush oasis, which was watered by a small body of water. The marabout told the others to wait for him on the valley ridge while he made sure it was safe. He was not surprised to find traces of jinn in the valley, and rushed back to inform the Gaawo virgins. It was too late, however. The women could not resist visiting the oasis, and they had pitched their tent on the water's edge. They were tired and refused to move. Soon the women fell fast asleep.

During the night, Maghegh — a powerful jinni who spent most of his time in the water — rose up like a thick dark mist and entered the bodies of each of the women. Meanwhile, the marabout dreamed that the virgins were being visited by a strange and magical spirit but that he was unable to help them. In the morning, the marabout woke knowing each woman was pregnant with a son.

Above: *A group of Tuareg nomadic traders, like their ancestors the Gaawo brides of the powerful jinn Maghegh, cross the inhospitable desert on camels.*

Instead of completing their journey, the group stayed at the oasis to give birth to their sons. With the help of their learned guide, the young mothers raised their sons and taught them reading, writing, riding, woodwork, leatherwork, and other skills that they needed to prosper. Their jinni father, Maghegh, met with his sons in the desert from time to time and taught them magical skills. The boys grew up to be brave and resourceful warriors. They fought and worked for local chiefs, who rewarded them with wives. In this way, the descendants of Maghegh's seven virgin "wives" prospered and grew in number, forming the main clans of the Tuareg.

Saharan Nomadic Life

In size and difficulty of crossing, the Sahara Desert has been compared to an ocean. Yet it has not prevented West Africans, such as the Tuareg, from building links with the wider world.

The story of Maghegh's wives places the origin of the Tuareg in a remote oasis in the vast Sahara. For thousands of years the Tuareg and other nomadic peoples have lived in and crossed the desert, trading goods from north to south. The Tuareg's real ancestors, the Berbers, were the first people to inhabit the north of Africa.

By the time the region was conquered by Arabs in the 8th century, the Berbers had broken into different groups, including the Tuareg, who gradually moved southward. By the 20th century, Tuaregs lived in what is now northern Mali and Niger in western Africa, and southern Algeria and Libya in North Africa. Today the Tuareg, who still speak a Berber language, include black Africans and Arabs among their ancestors.

The Tuareg perfected their desert-living skills over many centuries. They bred camels and kept large herds of goats, sheep, and cattle. Rarely staying in one place for long, they moved from one water hole or temporary pasture to the next to feed and water their animals. Pasture was provided by patches of grass that sprung up in the dry grasslands after infrequent rains, and fertile pockets

Above: *Tuareg women and some children join together in a festival of music making and storytelling.*

(oases) in the desert provided resting places and water. Many Tuareg have been forced to settle in one place since colonial borders carved up their lands.

Different Tuareg groups have different myths of origin, but they generally involve women as the founding ancestors. Individual Tuaregs still trace their descent through their mother. A man will identify himself as the son of a woman from a certain clan, for example. Tuareg chiefs are succeeded by their sons or their sister's sons.

Women owned the nomads' mobile homes: tents that could be dismantled and packed on a camel. Loose, flowing clothes seem too hot for desert life, but in fact they keep the wearer from losing too much water in sweat and keep sunlight off the skin. A Tuareg man would wear a long veil called a

Above: *A Tuareg man wearing the traditional blue veil to cover his face.*

tagelmust wrapped around his head and over his face. This veil was usually colored a deep blue with indigo dye. Some of the dye would rub off on the wearer's face, giving the Tuareg their nickname of "Blue Men." It was considered rude for a man to show his face. Unlike many other Muslim women, Tuareg women were not expected to cover their faces.

Sultan of Air

The Tuareg are one of many West African peoples who grew rich trading across the vast Sahara Desert. While most Africans benefited by controlling the trade depots at either side of the desert, desert nomads such as the Tuareg were perfectly placed to control the trade routes themselves. Huge caravans of Tuareg travelers carried gold, slaves, ebony, and ivory north from mighty West African states such as historic Ghana, Mali, and then Songhay. Grain, weapons, glass, cotton, and salt were carried south across the desert.

The Tuareg also prospered by levying taxes on goods that passed through their lands. Sometimes there were disputes over control of the lucrative trans-Saharan trade. So, in the early 15th century, elders of the seven Tuareg clans elected a sultan to preside over disputes. Based in Agadez, the Sultan of Air, as the new ruler became known, governed an area that, at its greatest extent in the 19th century, stretched north to Libya and south to northern Nigeria.

The Emperor and the Magician

At the start of the 19th century Seku Ahmadu (1775–1844) founded the Muslim state of Macina, located in modern Mali. One of his aims was to bring more converts to Islam.

SEKU AHMADU RESOLVED to wipe out the remaining traces of all other religions, leaving only Islam as the one true belief. Although many of the people living in that region — the Bambara and Songhay, for example — were already Muslim, they still consulted with priests associated with ancient local water spirits, called jinn (or genies).

Seku Ahmadu declared that any priest who did not turn to Islam would be executed. But he did not want to appear unjustly cruel, so he gave them a test to prove if the powers they claimed were real. One priest, Waada Samba, was known far and wide as a man of great powers. He lived to the north of Seku Ahmadu's capital on an island in a great pool. Stories of the miracles Waada performed reached Ahmadu, who sent an impressive cavalry to collect the old man.

Ahmadu ordered his most-trusted servants to catch a guinea fowl (an African pheasant) and enclose it in a lidded pot so that no one could tell what was inside. Then, he summoned all the Muslim holy men — the marabouts — and Waada and his followers. He told the assembled wise men, "Use your powers to divine what is in this pot; he who lies will have his throat cut." The marabouts were the first to try. After much discussion and divining, one of them said, "The animal has four paws." Another added, "...and large ears…" A third concluded. "It's a hare!" Seku Ahmadu was very disappointed with their answer, but he remained calm and gave no sign.

Waada Samba began to dance around the pot, until he fell into a trance — half awake and half unconscious, he communicated with his jinn. Waada emerged from the trance to declare forcefully, "The animal has two feet, wings, and is black with white spots.... It's a guinea fowl."

Seku Ahmadu was in a dilemma. If the people of his new state learned that the marabouts had been outwitted by a local priest, they were unlikely to abandon their old beliefs. Ahmadu prayed to Allah (God), "Make this priest into a liar so light can triumph over darkness."

Seku Ahmadu lifted the lid off the pot and out leapt a small hare. The animal skittered across the ground for several yards, then transformed back into a guinea fowl and flew away. It was decided that although the local priest had told the truth, Allah was always right.

Above: *Although the priest Waada Samba predicted correctly that inside Seku Ahmadu's pot was a guinea fowl, Allah, in answer to the Muslim ruler's prayers, briefly turned the bird into a hare.*

Countries along the Mighty Niger River

The Niger River has been called the Nile of West Africa for its fertile shores and important historical role. Many powerful nations arose on its banks, including two of the largest ever in Africa — Mali and Songhay.

Macina, where Seku Ahmadu prayed to Allah to help convert his people to Islam, lay in modern Mali. Centuries earlier Mali had been one of Africa's most powerful empires. Its wealth was based on the fertile farmland and easy transport provided by the Niger River. The Niger rises in central Guinea then travels in a gigantic arc through Mali, southwestern Niger, then Nigeria to reach the Atlantic Ocean. At 2,600 miles (4,200 km) long, it is the

Above: *The Niger River is the major waterway through West Africa. Here the long river runs through Mali.*

third-longest river in Africa. On its route, the river passes through nearly all the landscape types of West Africa, including the semidesert Sahel, the Sahara, rain forest, grasslands, highlands, marshes, and mangrove swamps.

For a 300-mile (480-km) stretch in central Mali, the river splits into many channels, becoming a dense network of creeks, swamps, lakes, and pools dotted with sandbanks and islands. The annual flooding of this massive inland delta has made it one of the most fertile places in Africa. The river itself has long provided seasonal transport links with lands in the forests to the south, where many of the historic gold-producing regions are, and with trade routes traveling north across the Sahara Desert.

Historically, a succession of powerful states dominated the lands along the Niger River. The ancient empire of Ghana (see page 13) arose to the east of the river but drew some of its power

from control of trading cities such as Tombouctou (formerly Timbuktu), which was then positioned on the north bank of the Niger River where it passed though the desert.

A small West African kingdom called Kangaba was based on the river south of its inland delta, just north of what is now the Guinea border. It was founded around 750 by Mandingo-speaking people. In 1224, all members of the ruling family were killed by Susu invaders. All, that is, apart from one crippled prince called Sundiata (died 1255), who was spared since he was not considered a threat. This proved to be a mistake. Sundiata, who earned the nickname "Lion of Mali," was a great hunter and soldier. By 1240 he had conquered the Susu and what was left of the empire of Ghana, bringing the empire of Mali into existence.

MAGNIFICENT MUSA

Mali grew rich by controlling goldfields in the south and the gold-trade routes

Above: *This kaba-blon (shrine) in modern Mali is dedicated to the Keita clan, whose ancestor was Sundiata, founder of the Mali empire.*

Below: *A 14th-century map of northern Africa. Mansa Musa is depicted as a European-style king.*

to the north. By the 1330s, under the ruler Mansa Musa (around 1264–1337), Mali reached its largest extent, covering present-day Senegal, Gambia, Guinea-Bissau, most of modern Mali, parts of Mauritania, and even southern Algeria. At that time, West Africa supplied most of Europe's gold, and the fame of kings such as Mansa Musa reached far beyond the continent.

Musa was a devout Muslim, and in 1324 he went on a pilgrimage to Mecca. Passing through Egypt on the way, he spent so much gold that he devalued the Egyptian currency; Arab historians wrote of the event and the king's glittering retinue for years.

Mali declined after Musa's death. It was eclipsed by the Songhay empire in 1340. Songhay existed as a small state founded by the Songhay people as early as 750. Its capital was Gao, a city on the Niger River east of its great bend in what is now north-central Mali. Sunni Ali (1464–1492) made Songhay the most powerful empire in West Africa, and his successor, Askia Muhammad (1493–1528), made it one of the world's largest at that time. The empire ended when it was conquered by Morocco in 1591.

Two Brothers Quarrel

The Fon people of modern Benin worship a host of vodun, or gods, and a supreme god, Mawu-Lisa. This myth explains how Sagbata came to reign over the earth vodun, and Sogbo over those of thunder, lightning, rain, and storms.

AFTER MAWU-LISA created the universe, including earth, she told her sons, Sagbata and Sogbo, to rule the world on her behalf. But the brothers could never agree, and they were always arguing. After a very bad argument, the eldest brother, Sagbata, decided to leave the sky for earth.

Mawu-Lisa was very disappointed that her sons were not able to rule together. She told them of her disapproval and of her decision that Sagbata should be the lord of all her wealth on earth. Sogbo would control thunder and the fire of the lightning bolt. She ordered both to live in the world, but Sogbo refused to leave his mother.

When Sagbata moved to the earth he packed many precious treasures in his large travel bag. But he left water and fire behind because they would have soaked or burned all the treasures he carried with him. The journey to earth was difficult, and Sagbata realized he would never be able to return home.

With Sagbata far away, Sogbo gained the confidence of his mother and the other sky gods. He knew that he could do whatever he wanted to prove he was more powerful than his brother, so he stopped the rain from falling on earth.

The people on earth had made Sagbata their king. Now, however, they regretted that decision. "As long as you have been king, there has been no rain. Our crops won't grow, and our animals can't eat or drink. We are dying," they complained. Sagbata assured them it would soon rain. Three rainless years passed, however.

Sagbata learned of two sky spirits who were diviners who had come to earth to teach divination, or *fa*. When someone wanted to ask the gods a question, the diviners would throw seeds of prophecy on the ground and read the answer in the patterns formed. Sagbata summoned the diviners. He told them how he had left water behind but now needed it for life on earth. They told Sagbata that if he wanted it to rain again, he would have to make friends with his brother.

Sagbata did not know what to do. He could not meet with his brother, since he lived in the sky. The diviners told him to summon Wututu, Sogbo's messenger bird, who could take a message to Sogbo. Sagbata summoned Wututu,

Above: *Rain is essential to all farming areas of West Africa, which is why the Fon people believe it is important to keep the deity-brothers Sogbo and Sagbata happy with each other.*

and told the bird that he would let Sogbo rule his part of the universe if Sogbo allowed rain to fall once more. Wututu flew up into the heavens to speak with Sogbo.

When Sogbo heard the message, he was very pleased. "Tell my brother," he said to the bird, "that, although he is the elder, he was foolish to leave behind the two things that power the universe — fire and water. Nevertheless, I accept his offer." Before Watutu had even reached earth, it began to rain. Sogbo and Sagbata have remained friends ever since, and this is why rain, thunder, and lightning visit earth once a year during the rainy season.

Voodoo and Slavery

Today African influences exist throughout the Americas, one result of the inhuman slave trade. In Brazil and the islands of the Caribbean, people follow religions that are clearly derived from the Fon and Yoruba belief systems.

West Africans, indeed all peoples, developed belief systems that helped explain the existence of nature and gave the believers a feeling of control of it. This, of course, was especially important in the parts of the world, such as West Africa, where the extremes of weather have such a profound effect on agriculture. This explains why deities including Sagbata, who ruled over earth, and Sogbo, who commanded the weather, held prime positions in the Fon religion.

Above: *This painting shows enslaved Africans in the early 19th century. The slave trade was so profitable that Africans captured other Africans for money and guns.*

From the 16th to the 19th centuries, more than six million enslaved Africans were shipped from the west coast of Africa to the Americas. They took their religious belief systems with them. The journey from Africa was horrifying. Hundreds of people were crammed into leaky vessels, and many died during the perilous Atlantic crossing. Those that survived were bought and sold like cattle and forced to spend the rest of their lives working for white owners.

Slavery and an internal slave trade had existed in West Africa for centuries, but never before had so many people been enslaved. The lucrative trade lured some Africans into supplying slaves. Wars were increasingly waged to gain captives, who were sold to slave traders at the coast.

PRACTICING OLD BELIEFS

Officially African slaves were forced to abandon their cultural practices, but in secret they kept hold of their religious beliefs. Over the centuries these beliefs merged with other religions. The

Haitian voodoo, for example, is based on the Fon religion. Many Haitians worship gods called *loa*, who often relate directly to Fon vodun. Legba and Sogbo (see box) exist in both Haiti and Benin, where the Fon live.

Devotees of the *loa* contact the gods to ask for their help, taking offerings of food and drink to please them. Sometimes a devotee will be possessed by the god and adopt his or her mannerisms, perhaps smoking a cigar or supping the god's favorite drink.

Above: *A modern voodoo ritual in Haiti. By performing such rituals these descendants of enslaved Africans are in part keeping alive the rituals and beliefs of their African ancestors.*

The name voodoo has negative meanings based on centuries of misunderstanding. Since the slaves were forced to practice their religion in secret, an aura of mystery surrounded their rituals, and that sense of mystery was heightened by the ignorance of whites concerning African religions in general. The wooden figures that Fon people used to communicate with their vodun were labeled fetishes or idols by the whites, since Europeans thought the carvings themselves were the Fon's gods. These figures were banned, but people made smaller ones out of cloth that they could easily hide. This is the origin of so-called voodoo dolls.

The Fon Religion

The supreme god of the Fon religion is Mawu-Lisa, who created earth before withdrawing to the sky (see page 22). Mawu-Lisa, the "soul of the world," is both man and woman. Mawu is the feminine side, representing fertility, motherhood, the moon, night, and calm. Lisa is the masculine side, representing power, war, the sun, day, and heat. Together, they bring balance to the universe. The numerous vodun (children of Mawu-Lisa) are branches of her power, each appointed to control a certain aspect of the world. After Sogbo, Hevioso is the most powerful of the thunder gods. Gu is the god of iron, associated with warfare, machinery, and technology. Mami-wata, "mother of water," is a relatively new but popular vodu in both the Americas and Africa. Legba is the messenger of the gods; anyone who wishes to communicate with the other vodun must first speak with Legba.

Left: *A Fon figure embodying magic power from the vodun.*

Anansi and the Rubber Man

In the forested West African state of Ghana, stories are told about the spider Anansi, a famous trickster whose exploits are known as far afield as the Caribbean and North America.

LIKE ALL TRICKSTERS, Anansi the Spider knows how to use his cunning and intelligence to overcome much larger and stronger opponents. Sometimes, however, even Anansi learns a painful, or in this case embarrassing, lesson.

Anansi the Spider was lazy. The people of Anansi's village worked hard to grow peanuts and other crops, but not Anansi. Every day, he got up at noon to eat his breakfast, then left the house. "I'm going to our farm," he would lie to his wife. Anansi did no work on his farm, though. Instead, he spent the afternoons lounging under a tree.

When it was time to plant new crops Anansi's wife was worried because her husband had not bought any seeds. Eventually, after he could delay planting no longer, Anansi asked his wife to visit the market and buy some nuts for him. The next day, Anansi made a big fuss about taking the nuts to his farm. He did not plant the nuts but spent the day under his favorite tree eating them. Anansi finished the whole sack of nuts without planting a single one.

For a while, things continued as normal. Anansi would rise at midday, eat his breakfast, then "go to the farm." Then harvest time arrived. The villagers were busy harvesting their nuts. "Where are our nuts?" Anansi's wife asked him again and again; she began to worry once more. One day, Anansi decided to steal someone else's nuts and pretend they were his. Late that night he crept out of his house and headed for the chief's farm, which he knew was large and full of ripe nuts. There he filled his bag with the chief's nuts and left it under his favorite tree. The next day, he told his wife, "I will harvest our nuts today." His wife was very pleased, and even more so when Anansi returned that evening with a bag of tasty nuts.

Greedy Anansi returned to the chief's farm several nights in a row. The chief's servant soon realized someone was stealing nuts, so he decided to set a trap to catch the thief. The servant went to the forest and tapped a rubber tree, collecting several basins of sticky sap. He used this to make a sticky rubber man, which he planted next to the chief's nut trees.

Anansi returned to the farm to steal more nuts. This time, he was surprised by the rubber man, which loomed out of the darkness at him. Startled and a bit scared, Anansi cried out, "Who

Above: *Anansi the Spider, a West African mythological trickster, is based both on observation of spiders that live in the region and on common human characteristics, such as laziness, greed, and cunning.*

are you? What are you doing here in the middle of the night?" There was no reply. "Why don't you answer me?" Anansi was getting angry, and he swung at the rubber man. His fist stuck. "Let go of me," he shouted, and raised his other fist. That, too, stuck to the rubber man. Anansi was desperate, and tried to push himself off with his feet — they stuck fast.

When the sun rose the next morning, Anansi's fear turned to shame. The chief's servant summoned the villagers to the farm, where they found Anansi glued to the rubber man, so everyone knew he was the thief. Ever since then Anansi and all his spider relatives have hidden away in dark corners because they are too embarrassed to show their faces.

Trickster Tales and Fables

As well as Anansi the Spider, Tortoise and Hare are popular tricksters in West Africa. Tricksters and other animals appear in fables, which are stories told to teach and entertain.

Nearly all cultures around the world have mythical tricksters, such as Anansi the Spider in West Africa and Coyote for many Native Americans. The Yoruba *orisha* (god) Eshu, and the Fon's Legba, are contrary characters; if forgotten in a person's prayers, they may take their revenge in unforeseen ways. Yet they are also sought out for protection, to do good deeds, or to bring harm to someone's enemies.

More commonly, tricksters are animals that people think are clever and cunning, though they may not always approve of how they behave. Most tricksters are characters in fables. Fables are stories in which good behavior is generally rewarded with some kind of fortune, and bad behavior is punished with misfortune. Other animal fables explain the natural world that people live in — how the leopard got his spots, for example, or how the goat came to be domesticated (used by people).

Trickster tales often provide an interesting twist to fables. Though they do not always practice fair play, tricksters are admired for their resourcefulness and ability to beat the odds: they can outwit enemies who could otherwise easily destroy them.

The Igbo and Yoruba people of southern Nigeria tell stories of a tortoise trickster. He makes fools of animals much larger than himself, including the elephant. In a world-famous tale that came from West Africa, Tortoise challenges Hare to a race, and despite being much slower, Tortoise wins. Perhaps trickster tales

Above: *During royal occasions these two ivory leopards were placed on either side of the oba's throne. The "oba" is the king of historic Benin in Nigeria.*

are so popular in many parts of the world because they give hope to those in society who feel oppressed or are viewed as being weak.

When Africans were enslaved and shipped to the Americas (see page 24), those who survived the death-ridden Atlantic crossing kept their languages, music, cultures, myths, and fables alive. American-born Africans adapted these fables and more-familiar American animals replaced those of Africa — Hare with Rabbit, for example. Anansi the Spider survived the crossing, however, and flourishes in the Caribbean.

REMUS AND BRER RABBIT

In 1880 Joel Chandler Harris (1848–1908) published *Uncle Remus: His Songs and His Sayings*. White, Georgia-born Harris wrote the stories after reading about African folklore. Uncle Remus, a wise black slave, told stories about Brer (Brother) Rabbit, who repeatedly outwits the fiercer Brer Fox, Brer Wolf, and Brer Bear. Writers continue to invent fables, and reinvent existing ones. Several West Africans have worked old and new mythical themes into their literature, including Nobel Prize winner Wole Soyinka.

The Ashanti Empire

Though many West African fables tell of spider tricksters, Anansi the Spider originally belonged to the Akan-speaking people of south-central Ghana. The most famous Akan people are the Ashanti, whose centuries-old state became a powerful empire in the 18th century. Its wealth was based on trading in gold and slaves, and the well-organized Ashanti army was difficult to defeat. Despite great resistance, the Ashanti were conquered by the British in the early 1900s.

The Ashantihene's (king's) symbol of authority was a golden stool that descended from heaven. Although the Ashantihene was always a man, the queen mother (more often the sister of the king) was an important adviser and had great influence at court. Like

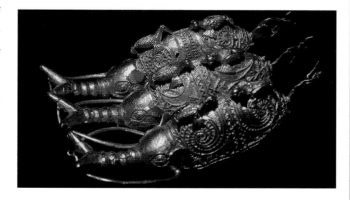

Above: *Three gold jewelry ornaments of elephants and birds, made by the Ashanti in the 19th-century.*

the Tuareg (see page 17), the Ashanti traced their ancestry through their mothers, and women elders were regarded as the main authority concerning family matters.

Sky-Food, Yams, and Cocoyams

Myths of the Igbo people of southeastern Nigeria encourage both individual achievement and responsibility to the community.

THE FIRST PEOPLE, Eri and his wife Namuaku, came from the sky. They were sent down to earth by the god Chukwu. At that time, most of the land was covered with water, and Eri was forced to perch on a termite mound when he arrived. Disappointed, Eri complained to Chukwu that there was nowhere to go, so Chukwu sent a blacksmith who used his fiery bellows to dry up the land.

Eri and Namuaku made earth their home, and they soon had children. The family lived on sky-food provided by Chukwu. They ate *azu igwe*, a fish that lived in the back of the sky. Because they ate sky-food, the family never needed to sleep.

When Eri died the food supply dried up, and Eri's children did not know how to farm — there were no crops for them to grow anyway. The eldest son, Nri, petitioned Chukwu about their lack of food. Chukwu told him to kill his firstborn son and firstborn daughter and bury them in separate graves. Nri did not want to kill any of his children, but pleading with Chukwu did not help. With great sadness, Nri killed his eldest daughter and son and buried them as commanded. After three Igbo weeks (12 days), Nri noticed plants sprouting from

the graves. Yams grew on the grave of his son and cocoyams on the grave of his daughter. Nri harvested the crops, and when his family ate the new foods, they slept for the first time.

Chukwu then instructed Nri to kill two slaves — a woman and a man — and bury them in separate graves, too. Again, after three Igbo weeks had passed, shoots were spotted sprouting from the graves. This time an oil palm grew on the man's grave and a breadfruit tree on the woman's. Nri's family lived well on their new food supplies.

Soon, though, Chukwu again commanded Nri to perform an unwelcome task: Nri must share the crops with the other people who now populated the earth. Nri was not eager to share the fruits of his painful sacrifices. After much debate, Nri and Chukwu reached a compromise. If Nri shared the food, Chukwu would grant him and his descendants privileges over his neighbors. This is how the Nri dynasty was founded. From that day on, the children of Nri — the Umunri — received tributes from their neighbors and, from Chukwu, the *ogwu-ji* (yam medicine), which ensures a good harvest every year for the people of Nri and those who acknowledge their rule.

Above: *An ancient Igbo deity carving, perhaps of Nri and his family enjoying their harvest, which was used in special rituals to encourage a good yam harvest. Yams are a staple of the Igbo diet.*

The Igbo Have No Kings

The Igbo are famous for the flexible, almost democratic nature of their society. Although considered one tribe, the Igbo were actually a collection of autonomous villages.

Below: *An Igbo ritual bowl from the 10th century. The bowl is made of bronze and is decorated with insects, but its precise use is uncertain.*

By adhering to the story of Nri and his crops (see page 30) the Igbo farmers segregated their cultivation. The men farmed the crops that grew from the graves of Nri's son and male slave — yams and oil palm — and the women farmed the crops that grew from the graves of Nri's daughter and female slave — cocoyams and breadfruit. The Igbo men's crops are considered more prestigious and are used in rituals like the yam festival. They were also once used as currency. The Igbo women's crops are more basic foodstuffs.

IGBO SELF-RULE

In Nigeria, an Igbo saying goes: *Igbo enwe eze*, meaning "The Igbo have no kings." This is true of the vast majority of Igbo people, who live east of the Niger River in Nigeria. The Nri dynasty emerged among the western Igbo, where several towns had different rulers. These kings could be dethroned by their people, and the position was usually awarded or inherited.

Most Igbo, however, did not have kings, and in the past they lived in highly structured societies in which many people had a voice. Each town had a policy-making body made up of elders, both women and men, age-grade leaders, and heads of titled societies. (An age-grade is a group of men or women who are initiated into adulthood together.) Decisions were made by consensus, so the majority had to agree. Igbo myths reflect this tradition of debate and ability to question authority: gods, for example, are not unquestioningly obeyed but can be argued with and challenged.

Status in Igbo society was linked to age, wealth, and personal achievement, not birthright. A woman who worked hard to feed her family and build up her wealth, for example, could earn respect and the title of *ekwe*, member of the Women's Council. Ambition at the expense of the community was not encouraged, and status brought responsibilities as well as privileges.

Left: *A 20th-century Igbo head-dress showing an enslaved Igbo woman being marched away by a European slave trader.*

Village self-rule suffered in the 20th century when the Igbo were conquered by the British. The British appointed local rulers who supported them, undermining the complex checks and balances of Igbo politics. They also assumed women had no independence, so limited their rights. The British later regretted this, however, when the Igbo women orchestrated a widespread revolt, known as the 1929 Women's War. Market traders burned foreign-owned factories and destroyed "Native Courts" set up by the British.

IGBO RELIGION

In the past, each Igbo had their own personal divinity, or *chi*. Sometimes called the "god within," a person's *chi* accompanied them throughout their life. People were protected and advised by their *chi*, to whom they prayed and made offerings. The personal basis of the Igbo religion fostered both individual responsibility and ambition. Today, many Christian Igbo still keep in touch with both their *chi* and the Christian God.

Igbo, Supreme God?

Chukwu (see page 30) is often called the supreme god of the Igbo. Many people disagree, while others who accept Chukwu as supreme god insist this is a recent development. Historically, every Igbo town had its own god or goddess associated with a particular place such as a cave or clearing in a forest. Townspeople used them as a court of last appeal, to predict the future, and to detect criminals.

Above: *The Igbo god Chukwu dwelled in an eerie cave.*

The Igbo of Aro region had a powerful god called Chukwu, who had a fearsome grotto. The Aro were prominent traders throughout the Igbo's lands, and they spread the fame of Chukwu. The Aro god mediated disputes from far afield. When the British arrived, they assumed Chukwu was the supreme god of the Igbo. In reality, every Igbo town had its own myth of origin, ancestry, and religious history.

Prince of Heaven

The spiritual heart of the ancient Yoruba religion has always been the city of Ife, now called Ile-Ife, located in southwest Nigeria. This myth explains why.

IN THE BEGINNING there was only the sky and the heavens above and water below. All the gods lived in the heavens, and they were ruled by the wisest and most powerful god, Olorun. The goddess Olokun reigned over the empty waters below heaven.

The gods paid little attention to the water below, but one day a young sky god named Obatala grew bored with the lack of living things there. Knowing that he was the chief god's favorite, Obatala asked Olorun if he could create land over some of the water so people and animals could roam on it. Olorun allowed Obatala to carry out his plan.

Obatala had no idea how to create land, so he went to see Orunmila (also called Ifa, the god of Divination), who was Prince of Heaven and eldest son of Olorun. Orunmila could see into the future and told Obatala to find enough gold to make a chain long enough to reach the waters below.

Joining together all the gold jewelry that belonged to the other gods, Obatala was able to make a chain that he thought was long enough. Next Orunmila told Obatala to fill a snail's shell with sand, and gather a white hen, a black cat, and a palm nut in a bag. After he had done this

the Prince of Heaven instructed Obatala to carry these things with him down the chain.

Orunmila watched over Obatala as he hooked one end of the gold chain to the edge of the sky and lowered the other toward the waters below. Obatala slung the bag over his shoulder and began the descent. He inched his way down the gold chain but it did not reach the water's surface; it ended far above, and Obatala swung there, unsure of what to do next. Orunmila called out, telling him to empty the sand from the snail's shell. Obatala took the shell from his bag and poured out the sand. Orunmila then said to release the white hen. Obatala did this, and the bird fluttered down to the sand. The hen scratched at the sand, scattering it all over. Instantly, small heaps of sand turned into hills and large piles of sand made mountains.

Obatala jumped onto the newly created land. He took the palm nut from his bag and planted it at the spot where he first landed. Obatala named the spot "Ife," in honor of the god of Divination. Obatala built a house, where he lived with the black cat for company. When Obatala later created children, Ife became the birthplace of humankind.

Left: *This carving is of an ancient unknown king of Ife. According to the Yoruba, Ife was the birthplace of humankind. The holes around the figure's mouth would have held strands of hair.*

Yoruba Kingdoms and Gods

The Yoruba of southwest Nigeria have been living in towns and cities for more than 1,000 years; they were the first urban people in West Africa.

Today there are more than 20 million Yoruba people living in parts of Benin and Togo as well as southwestern Nigeria. The different Yoruba groups are loosely linked by geography, language, history, and religion. For centuries, the Yoruba have lived in towns and cities. Obatala's Ife (now Ile-Ife), historically the first Yoruba town, could have been founded as early as A.D. 850. It was named for the god of Divination Ifa (or Orunmila, Prince of Heaven, see page 34).

Other towns followed, and each was ruled by a king, called the *alafin* in Oyo and the *oni* in Ife. The *alafins* of Oyo claimed descent from Oduduwa (a son of Olorun, the high god). Though Oyo became an empire, Ife has always remained the center of the Yoruba religion. When an *alafin* of Oyo was enthroned, he had to swear not to attack Ife. One *alafin* who raided Ife for slaves in the 1790s almost began a civil war.

Yoruba towns generally had a distinctive wheel-shaped layout. Many of their citizens were farmers who left the town to work their land, but many were also traders, specialist craft workers, or officials. Several Yoruba cities became flourishing trading and political centers, including Oyo by the 14th century, Ilorin by the 18th century, and Ibadan by the 19th century.

IFE WORKS OF ART

The 14th century was a period of prosperity for Ife, and many famous works of art were produced for the royal court, shrines, and nobles. The kingdom of Benin, whose citizens were the Edo-speaking Bini, lay to the east. Benin was greatly influenced by Ife. Ife sculptors produced beautiful, realistic human heads in terra-cotta, and Ife metalworkers perfected the art of lost-wax casting to make intricate brass castings. Metalcasters made wax

Above: *A 17th-century sculpture of Orunmila, also known as Prince of Heaven and god of Divination.*

Left: *The oba (ruler) of the kingdom of Benin, which may have been founded by a Yoruba prince. The oba, Akenzua XI, pictured here in 1964, is dressed in full royal regalia, including a coral headdress worn only on special occasions.*

models that they covered in clay and dried, then melted the wax so it could be poured out, leaving a perfect mold.

OLD AND NEW

Oyo (now Old Oyo) became an empire by conquering neighboring states and dominated a large region from 1650 to the early 19th century. After Ilorin declared independence in 1817, the empire began to disintegrate. Wars between the Yoruba states raged for much of the 19th century. Ibadan, founded by military and civilian refugees from Oyo, took over much of the territory formerly ruled by the empire. It was nominally governed by the *alafin* of Oyo, now based at New Oyo, but real power lay with the military commander of Ibadan.

By 1914, however, the Yoruba kingdoms had all been defeated by the British and forced to join the Protectorate (colony) of Nigeria. Yoruba kings still exist but their roles are largely ceremonial, they have little real power.

Yoruba Gods

The host of Yoruba gods has been compared to the pantheons of ancient Greece and Rome. There is one overall god, Olorun (or Olodumare), and several hundred deities called *orishas*. Although the high god has no dedicated priests, the *orishas* are extensions of Olorun, and the messenger god Eshu can deliver offerings people make to Olorun. Eshu, sometimes called the trickster god, can cause trouble for those who neglect him or the other *orishas*.

Some *orishas* have been in existence before earth, while others were once real heroes. Shango, the *orisha* of thunder, was a king of Oyo famed for his skills as a warrior and a magician who could control thunder and lightning. Other important *orishas* include Olokun (goddess of waters) and Ogun (god of iron, war, and technology).

Left: *A Yoruba staff used in special religious ceremonies to represent Shango, the* orisha *(god) of thunder.*

The Mermaid and the Chameleon

Many West African people tell a similar version of this myth. In this Igbo version, the water goddess, or Mermaid, is outwitted by Chameleon.

MERMAID, QUEEN OF the Oceans, Lakes, and Seas, felt she should be the supreme god, not Chukwu. The other gods encouraged her vanity and suggested she should arrange some sort of contest with Chukwu. Mermaid was regarded by all creatures, people, and gods as the most beautiful, sophisticated, and fashionable being of all. So she declared that a contest should be held to decide whether she or Chukwu was the best dressed. Chukwu was amused by her plans, but he agreed to join in and a day was set.

The day of the contest arrived. Mermaid put on a gorgeous dress and prepared for the contest. Mermaid had woven the cloths for her dresses herself so she could be sure of their quality. Chukwu sent Chameleon to fetch the water goddess. Being a creature of the water, Mermaid did not know Chameleon was able to change appearance at will. When she arose from her ocean palace to go with Chameleon, she was horrified to see that the animal wore the same outfit as her. She thought it did not bode well if the god's messenger was dressed as well as her. "I cannot wear the same clothes as a mere spectator

of the contest," the water goddess thought. Mermaid returned to her palace to change. This time she chose a beautiful outfit made of coral beads and put on some expensive jewelry.

More confident, Mermaid returned to her palace gate to meet Chameleon. A great surprise awaited her: Chameleon was once more wearing the same outfit as her. Mermaid rushed inside again to change. This time she wore the most expensive and elaborate clothes she owned; they were covered in rich embroidery and spun from golden thread. No one could be better dressed. But to her dismay, Chameleon still wore the same clothes as her. The cloth was as finely woven, and the embroidery as elaborately designed.

This time, Mermaid gave up the contest. "If his messenger is so well dressed, how much better dressed must Chukwu be," the water goddess thought. Since then, no other god has dared to challenge Chukwu.

In a similar myth, the Yoruba water goddess, Olokun (see page 34), gets involved in much the same type of difficulty. She challenges the supreme god Olorun to a cloth-making contest but is also defeated by the changeable Chameleon.

Left: *The story of Chameleon, the West African spirit who can change his appearance to mimic what others are wearing, is based on the amazing ability of real chameleons to change their skin color. This gives these lizards the advantage of being able to camouflage themselves both from prey and predators.*

Making Textiles

Making textiles has long been an important economic and artistic activity in West Africa. Today, work or everyday clothes are mostly imported, but luxury robes and other cloths are still produced to wear at special occasions.

For many West Africans appearance is very important. As in most cultures around the world, how one dresses can say a lot about that person's social status. The Igbo myth of Mermaid being outwitted by Chukwu and Chameleon (see page 38) shows not only that the gods can be vain but that clothes hold a special place in West African culture. Similarly, a myth of the Mossi people of Sierra Leone relates how their founding ancestor was a weaver who descended to earth

Above: *A West African man weaving textiles on a traditional loom.*

on the threads from his loom. Despite competition from mills, hand-spun Mossi cloth is still sought after and is passed down from parent to child.

Many West African cloths are still valued for their historical and ceremonial importance. Once worn only by Ashanti kings and now the national dress of Ghana, *kente* cloth is distinctive for its intricate patterns made from multicolored threads, often with gold as the dominant color. In Yoruba the kings dressed in robes and crowns made from thousands of coral beads.

The Ewe people of Togo and Ghana are famous weavers, and they make a cloth similar to *kente* called *keta*. Patterns are created by using different-colored warp (lengthwise) and weft (widthwise) threads. Like a lot of West African cloths, *keta* is woven in narrow strips that are then sewn together to make much wider fabrics. Strips range from less than 0.5 inches (12 mm) wide to nearly a yard.

Weavers, generally men, used a variety of threads to make their cloth.

Locally grown and hand-spun cotton was the most common thread. In what is now Nigeria, silk was harvested from the cocoons of wild moths that breed on tamarind trees. The Ashanti people first used silk unraveled from imported fabrics. Fibers of the raffia palm leaf can be made into threads but are more often kept in loose strips to make costumes such as those worn at masquerades (see pages 44–45). Fulani herders were among the few who weaved with wool. Since the 20th century, Lurex and other modern threads have been used to make cloths shine and sparkle.

Some materials are not woven at all but made from compressed plant fibers. This includes the barkcloth once traded by the Ashanti.

EMBELLISHING THE CLOTH

The long flowing gowns worn by West African men and women are often decorated with dense borders of embroidery around the neck and cuffs. Embroidery is still generally a male occupation, but many embroiderers now use sewing machines to complete their work much more quickly.

The Fon people have perfected the art of appliqué, in which fabric shapes are sewn onto a contrasting background to build up a picture. In the past, appliqué cloths were made to celebrate battles and kings, and depict Fon gods. Today, they are just as likely to feature social commentary.

Above: *A West African heddle pulley. The heddle are the cords that form the frame of the cloth on a loom.*

Right: *Chiefs gather for a festival in Ghana. For the special occasion the chiefs are wearing gold jewelry and their finest robes with distinctive designs.*

Dyes, especially the blues of the indigo plant, have a long history in West Africa. In the 15th and 16th centuries, many West African textiles were far better than those made in Europe. In particular, treatments used to fix dyes were much more advanced.

Dyes can be used to pattern cloth after it is made. In West Africa, women would tie, stitch, or paint with starch or wax the parts of the cloth they did not want to dye. This is called "resist dyeing," and it includes tie-dyeing and batiks.

In the past, Bambara men wore cloths woven by men but decorated by women. The Bambara women soak the cloth in dyes made from crushed leaves and bark. This turns the cloth dark brown or black. Then, the designer paints a pattern on the cloth with mud, ash, and vegetable oil. When the cloth is dry, the woman scrapes the mud off. The dye comes off in the places were the mud was applied, leaving a pale pattern on the dark background.

Dancing with Spirits

Until recently, most women in Sierra Leone belonged to a Sande society, which prepared girls for adulthood. Myths such as this one are narrated by Sande elders to instill certain virtues in new recruits.

ONE YEAR, THE SANDE society of a big town was holding a masquerade. Sande groups regularly hold masquerades and other dances to celebrate special occasions such as the coming out of young women newly initiated into the society. Four spirits in the heavens learned of the masquerade, and decided that they wanted to attend. Using a long rope, they climbed down to earth, where they dressed themselves handsomely.

The dance lasted for four days, and the spirits enjoyed themselves. They met four young women, who liked the spirits a lot. When the masquerade came to an end, though, it was time for the spirits to return home. The women begged to return with them, but the spirits knew they would not like life in the heavens. They warned them that there would be many sick and poor people. For one whole night the couples argued the matter. Finally, two of the girls were convinced. They pleaded with their lovers to return, and the young men said, "We will come here whenever a big dance is held." With that the women had to be satisfied.

The four spirits and two other women climbed the rope to heaven. The spirit Hawudui's young woman refused to help relieve the suffering of the sick people she met there, while Nyandebo's girlfriend was happy to wash their sores. The women stayed in the heavens until they became homesick, and they told their lovers' friends of their wish to return home. The friends warned the women that they would be tested before they left heaven: "Choose an old, worn box not a shiny new one," they advised mysteriously.

Nyandebo and Hawudui agreed to let the women return home, but first they told their chief. He summoned the women, and arranged for a mismatched collection of boxes to be spread on the ground before them. "Choose a box to take with you," the chief ordered. Hawudui's girlfriend chose the shiniest of all the boxes, but Nyandebo's girlfriend chose the oldest and most battered box.

The girls returned home with their prizes. When Nyandebo's friend unpacked her box, she drew out all kinds of riches. She shared their wealth with her family and all the town's dancers. They had so many riches they were able to start trading.

Left: *The tradi-
tional black mask
worn by senior
female officials of
the women-only
Sande society.
The women wear
the masks during
masquerades held
to mark the passage
of young girls
into adulthood.*

When Hawudui's girlfriend reached her house, she called all her relatives inside. "Shut the doors, and I will show you unimaginable riches," she boasted before asking her father to open the box. As soon as he removed the lid, a leopard leaped out and killed him. It was followed by lions and all kinds of fierce creatures, which ate everyone inside the house, then escaped to the bush. Like the ancient Greek myth of Pandora releasing from a box all the evils that plague humankind, so it is, thanks to one woman's stubbornness, that there are so many dangerous creatures in the world today. But, it is due to another woman's wise behavior that the Mende became traders.

Masks and Masquerades

In West Africa masked dancers perform at masquerades to entertain and celebrate, as well as appease or even mock spirits, seek out wrongdoers, and reinforce good behavior.

Visitors to museums of human history will be familiar with the great variety of masks, mostly wooden, produced by West African sculptors. Few of the masks are older than the 19th century, but they are part of a long history of mask making. West African masks vary greatly depending on the area or group. Some peoples make masks shaped like wild animals, while others are more fantastical and imaginative, with intricate carvings and contorted expressions.

Yet these masks are only one part of an elaborate performance art; they were designed to be worn by dancers wearing costumes at masquerades, often accompanied by musicians, drummers, and singers. Historically, the masquerades were held for a range of reasons, from celebrating victory in a battle to honoring the gods. During recent times the masquerades have been increasingly performed simply to entertain.

A masked dancer at a masquerade can represent a spirit, god, ancestor, or even a particular person or group of people. The Bambara people of Mali, for

Left: *Bambara dancers perform the traditional dance of thanks to Tyi-wara, the god who taught the Bambara how to farm. The dancers are wearing masks and costumes symbolic of the deity Tyi-wara, who was half-man and half-antelope.*

example, traditionally wore masks in the shape of antelopes during a masquerade held yearly to honor the god Tyi-wara — half-man, half-antelope — who taught the Bambara how to farm.

Yoruba Gelede masquerades, on the other hand, although performed by men, celebrate and appease women. Yoruba women manage their own financial affairs, run their own businesses (often as traders), and can easily earn more than their husbands.

masquerades. Only expert dancers can wear the mask of Sowo, the chief Sande spirit, who appears at the coming-out ceremonies of new members. The mask represents ideals of feminine beauty and behavior, with glossy black skin, intricate plaits, and a composed expression. Comic characters wearing old, ugly masks daubed with paint misbehaved and disrupted the occasion.

Gelede masquerades acknowledge the power women have to give and take life, while warning against the misuse of that power for evil deeds by witches.

"SECRET" SOCIETIES

Masquerades are often associated with particular societies, such as the women's Sande and men's Poro societies of Sierra Leone. People have misleadingly called these "secret" societies. While Sande and Poro did have secrets known only to members, they were not underground movements as the term suggests. In the past, nearly all adult Mende would belong to one or the other. New recruits would spend several weeks or months housed by Sande or Poro in a camp in the bush. There, the societies passed on their community's knowledge concerning its history, religion, and codes of conduct, as well as technical skills such as how to diagnose and treat illnesses, farm, weave, spin, and how to dance and sing Sande songs.

Sande maskers were almost unique for being women; elsewhere it is normally men who perform in the

Above: *Women gather around a masked dancer who is performing the initiation rite for the Sande society.*

Right: *The colorful and popular Rio Carnival in Brazil, which regularly draws millions of spectators, is a descendant of traditional African masquerades.*

THE NEW WORLD

These creative traditions have re-emerged in displaced African cultures, giving rise to some of the most spectacular carnivals in the world today. Africans enslaved and transported to the Americas were forbidden to practice their own religions. Masquerading continued, though, at first with Christian saints replacing African deities and spirits. Today, the carnivals of Rio (Brazil), Trinidad, and Notting Hill (London, England) are a vibrant and ever-developing legacy of these traditions.

Glossary

Anansi the Spider A famous trickster who, in one myth, was caught lying and being lazy.

Askia Muhammad Succeeded **Sunni Ali** and made Songhay one of the most powerful empires in West Africa.

azu igwe In Igbo mythology, a fish that lived in the back of the sky. It was eaten by **Eri**'s family.

Bida In Soninke mythology, the giant snake that guarded **Wagadu**.

Blue Men Term used for Tuareg men because of the stained blue dye on their faces. The dye comes off the scarves they wear to cover their faces, for Islamic religious reasons.

Chameleon In Igbo mythology, was summoned by **Chukwu** to defeat **Mermaid** in a duel to see who was the best dressed god.

chi An Igbo personal god or guardian spirit.

Chukwu In Igbo mythology he taught **Nri** how to grow the first crops. He was also challenged by **Mermaid** to see who was the better dressed of the two gods.

Dausi Epic poems or grand stories sung by Soninke **griots**.

Eri In Igbo mythology, the first man on earth, sent by **Chukwu**.

Eshu A Yoruba trickster god.

fa In Fon religion, the term for divination, or religious foresight.

griots West African chroniclers and storytellers.

Gu The god of iron, one of the Fon **vodun**.

Hawudui A spirit who attended the Sande masquerade, met a girl there, and allowed her to return to with him to the heavens. She chose a box there, but when her father opened it all the fierce creatures of the world were unleashed.

Hevioso A thunder god, one of the Fon **vodun**.

Ifa In Yoruba mythology, the Prince of Heaven, also called Orunmila, and eldest son of **Olorun**. He instructed **Obatala** on how to create **Ife**.

Ife A city now called Ile-Ife; in Yoruba mythology it was created by **Obatala** who named the place in honor of Orunmila (**Ifa**). The city is the spiritual center of the Yoruba religion.

Iyadola In Igbo mythology, a spirit woman created by **Nyame**. She made the first humans out of clay.

kente A patterned cloth, often embroidered with gold threads, that was the dress of Ashanti kings but is now the national costume of Ghana.

keta Similar to *kente*, it is made by the Ewe people of Togo and Ghana.

Kiloko In Soninke mythology, the buzzard that retrieved **Tabele** from the sky.

Lagarre Son of **Mama Dinga**, he made **Wagadu** visible.

Legba In Fon mythology, both a trickster god and the messenger of the **vodun**.

loa Haitian version of Fon **vodun**, or deities.

Maghegh A powerful jinni who was the father of the Tuareg people.

Mama Dinga An old king on Soninke whose son **Lagarre** made **Wagadu** visible.

Mamadi Sefe Dekote The killer of **Bida** and rescuer of **Sia Jatta Bari**. After he killed the giant snake the people of **Wagadu** turned on Mamadi and he was forced to flee.

Mami-wata Also called Mother of Water, a popular god, or **vodu**, in both Africa and the Americas.

Mansa Musa Emperor of Mali in the early 14th century and one of its greatest rulers.

marabouts Muslim holy men of great learning who were believed to have supernatural powers.

Mawu-Lisa In Fon mythology, the creator of the universe and mother of **Sagbata** and **Sogbo**.

Mermaid An Igbo goddess who challenged **Chukwu**.

Namuaku In Igbo mythology, the first woman and **Eri**'s wife.

Nri In Igbo mythology, **Eri**'s eldest son. He was instructed by **Chukwu** on how to grow the first yams, cocoyams, oil palm, and breadfruit. He was also founder of the Umunri people and the Nri dynasty.

Nyame In Igbo mythology, the Sky God who created all the plants, animals (except humans), and the sculptress **Iyadola**.

Nyandebo A spirit who, with his friend **Hawudui**, attended the Sande masquerade, met a girl there, and allowed her to return to with him to the heavens. His girlfriend chose a battered box from the heavens. When she opened it she found riches that she shared with her family and village.

Obatala In Yoruba mythology, a god who created the city of **Ife**. He was the favorite of **Olorun**.

ogwu-ji Yam medicine, which ensures a good harvest for **Nri** people and their followers.

Olokun In Yoruba mythology, the goddess of empty waters below heaven. She is similar to the Igbo goddess **Mermaid**.

Olorun In the Yoruba religion, ruler of the gods.

oni Title given to a ruler of **Ife**.

orisha The Yoruba name for a god.

Sagbata In Fon mythology, the brother of **Sogbo** and ruler of the earth's **vodun**.

Seku Ahmadu The first Muslim ruler of Masina, who asked Allah to trick **Waada Samba**.

seven Gaawo virgins In Tuareg mythology, the ancestral mothers of the Tuareg people.

Sia Jatta Bari A beautiful girl who lived in **Wagadu** and was to be sacrificed to **Bida**. She was rescued by **Mamadi Sefe Dekote**.

Sogbo In Fon mythology, the brother of **Sagbata** and ruler of thunder, lightning, rain, and storms.

Sultan of Air Title of the ruler of the Tuareg, based in Agadez.

Sundiata Founder of the Mali.

Sunni Ali 15th-century ruler of the Songhay empire.

Tabele In Soninke mythology, the great war drum that could make **Wagadu** visible.

Tyi-wara A god — half-man, half-antelope — who taught the Bambara people how to farm.

vodun In Fon religion, deity children of **Mawu-Lisa**, each controlling a different aspect of the world. A single one is called "vodu."

Waada Samba A non-Muslim priest who used his jinni to help him answer **Seku Ahmadu**'s challenge.

Wagadu A Soninke city that could magically appear and disappear.

Wututu The messenger bird of **Sogbo** who helped stop the fight between **Sagbata** and Sogbo and enabled the drought to end.

Further Reading & Viewing

BOOKS

Aardema, Verna, and Lisa Desimini. *Anansi Does the Impossible: An Ashanti Tale.* New York, NY: Aladdin, 2000.

Arkhurst, Joyce Cooper. *The Adventures of the Spider: West African Folktales.* Boston, MA: Little, Brown & Co., 1992.

Curtin, Philip D., ed. *Africa Remembered: Narratives by West Africans from the Era of the Slave Trade.* Prospect Heights, IL: Waveland Press, 1997.

Falola, Toyin. *The History of Nigeria.* Westport, CT: Greenwood Publishing Group, 1999.

Neimark, Philip John. *The World of the Orisa.* San Francisco, CA: HarperCollins, 1993.

VIDEOS

African Healing Dance. Sounds True Video, 1998.

In Search of History: Voodoo Secrets. A&E Video, 2000.

Sahara: A Place of Extremes. PBS Home Video, 2000.

West Africa. Lonely Planet, 1997.

WEBSITES

African Mythological Characters. http://www.cybercomm. net/~grandpa/mytlogy2.html.

Art & Life in Africa: Tuareg Information. http://www.uiowa. edu/~africart/toc/people/Tuareg.html.

West African Mythology. http://www.windows.ucar.edu/ cgi-bin/tour_def/mythology/african_culture.html.

Index